MW01156600

BECOMING LIKE GOD JOURNAL

For further information:

The Kabbalah Centre
155 E. 48th St., New York, NY 10017
1062 S. Robertson Blvd., Los Angeles, CA 90035

1.800.Kabbalah www.kabbalah.com

First Edition
December 2004
Printed in USA
ISBN 1-57189-365-2

Design: Hyun Min Lee

Dear Reader,

This is a book that will benefit you in a way that goes far beyond the usual objectives of self-help and personal development volumes. This book will help you to **BECOME LIKE GOD**.

What exactly does it mean to become like God, and how will this journal help you reach that goal? Simply put, by filling these blank pages with your thoughts and feelings, you will move closer to the ultimate happiness and fulfillment that is your true destiny. At the same time, it will help to free you from the chaos that is the root cause of all pain and suffering in your life.

In short, this journal is a framework in which you can discover your true potential for becoming a cause rather than an effect, for being proactive rather than reactive, and for creating your life rather than having it imposed upon you. Writing, after all, is a creative process. By writing about your life on a regular basis, with focused awareness and the conscious intention of becoming like God, you can be the creator of positive changes for yourself and for the world around you.

What will that require of you? Just a pencil or pen and the sincere desire for positive transformation. So if you've got those ready, let's get started.

Michael Berg

"THE TRUTH IS, WE ARE DESTINED TO BECOME LIKE GOD, BUT WE HAVE BEEN TRICKED INTO BECOMING INMATES OF A PRISON, INDIFFERENT TO THE GHASTLY SPREAD BETWEEN WHAT WE ARE AND WHAT WE COULD BE."

1. THINK BACK TO YOUR EARLY CHILDHOOD. WHAT WERE YOUR HOPES AND DREAMS? ARE YOU LIVING THEM TODAY? WHAT DID YOU WANT TO DO AND TO BE WHEN YOU WERE FIVE YEARS OLD, OR TEN, OR FIFTEEN? ARE YOU SATISFIED OR DISAPPOINTED WITH THE PERSON YOU ARE NOW COMPARED TO THE PERSON YOU WANTED TO BE? WRITE YOUR THOUGHTS BELOW.

2. IF YOUR LIFE CONTINUES ON ITS PRESENT PATH FOR THE NEXT TEN YEARS, WHERE DO YOU SEE IT LEADING? IN AS MUCH DETAIL AS POSSIBLE, PAINT A WORD PICTURE OF WHAT YOUR LIFE WILL BE LIKE A DECADE INTO THE FUTURE—PHYSICALLY, EMOTIONALLY, AND SPIRITUALLY. WHAT CHANGES DO YOU FORESEE? WHAT WILL REMAIN UNCHANGED?

3. HAS YOUR VISION OF THE FUTURE GROWN LARGER OR SMALLER DURING THE COURSE OF YOUR LIFE? WHEN YOU WERE A CHILD, WAS YOUR VISION CLOSER TO *BECOMING LIKE GOD* THAN IT IS AT PRESENT? IF SO, WHAT SPECIFIC THINGS CAN YOU DO NOW TO EXPAND AND ENLARGE YOUR EXPECTATIONS?

4. YOU HAVE THE SAME ESSENCE AND THEREFORE THE SAME POTENTIAL AS GOD. YOU ARE DESTINED TO BECOME LIKE GOD. DON'T JUST MEASURE YOURSELF AGAINST OTHER PEOPLE IN YOUR LIFE. MEASURE YOURSELF AGAINST GOD.

WHEN YOU ASK YOURSELF *"AM I LIKE GOD YET?"* WHAT ANSWERS DO YOU FIND? DOES THIS SEEM LIKE AN OUTRAGEOUS QUESTION? CAN YOU GRASP YOUR TRUE UNITY WITH THE CREATOR'S BEING? WRITE YOUR THOUGHTS BELOW.

5. *"IF YOU'RE NOT DOING WHAT YOU WERE MEANT TO DO—AND EACH PERSON WAS MEANT FOR SOMETHING ASTONISHING—YOU'LL NEVER ENJOY CONTENTMENT."*

WHAT ASTONISHING THINGS WERE <u>YOU</u> MEANT TO DO? IN THE SPACE BELOW, DESCRIBE THE TRULY GREAT THINGS YOU CAN DO WITH YOUR LIFE. DON'T WORRY ABOUT THE "REALISTIC" OBSTACLES THAT MIGHT GET IN YOUR WAY. LET YOUR THOUGHTS RUN FREE. WHAT WILL YOU DO TO REVEAL YOUR DIVINE DESTINY IN THE WORLD AROUND YOU?

"THE OPPONENT COMES DRESSED IN THE CLOTHES OF A FRIEND RATHER THAN IN THE UNIFORM OF A PRISON GUARD, AND THEN HE BETRAYS US TO OUR CAPTORS. EVEN WORSE, THE OPPONENT CONVINCES US THAT HE IS US. WHAT WE CALL LIFE IS A VAST CASE OF MISTAKEN IDENTITY, AND UNTIL WE DISTIN-GUISH OUR IDENTITY FROM THE OPPONENT'S, WE WILL REMAIN IMPRISONED."

1. *"THE NEGATIVE FORCE IN THE UNIVERSE IS CALLED DESIRE TO RECEIVE FOR THE SELF ALONE. IT IS ALSO KNOWN AS EGO NATURE, A FORCE THAT DOMINATES US VIRTUALLY ALL THE TIME—AND THIS FORCE IS THE SOURCE OF ALL OUR PAIN AND SUFFERING."*

WITH THIS QUOTE IN MIND, DESCRIBE A RECENT INCIDENT IN WHICH EGO PLAYED A MAJOR ROLE. DID YOU RECOGNIZE THE DESIRE TO RECEIVE FOR YOURSELF ALONE, OR WAS IT WELL DISGUISED AS SOME IMPORTANT REQUIREMENT OF THE EVERYDAY WORLD? LOOKING BACK, WHAT MAKES YOU ABLE TO RECOGNIZE IT NOW, AND HOW CAN THIS HELP YOU IN THE FUTURE?

2. *"WE BECOME LIKE GOD BY SYSTEMATICALLY DESTROYING THE EGO. THE DESIRE TO RECEIVE FOR THE SELF ALONE IS THE OPPOSITE OF GOD, BECAUSE GOD DOES NOT RECEIVE FROM ANYONE."*

HOW CAN YOU SYSTEMATICALLY DESTROY YOUR EGO DESIRES? WHAT CLEAR STEPS CAN YOU TAKE TODAY? IN THE NEXT WEEK? IN THE NEXT YEAR?

3. THINK OF A TIME WHEN YOU FELT SEVERELY HURT, DEEPLY EMBARRASSED, OR GRIEVOUSLY OFFENDED. AS YOU WRITE A DESCRIPTION OF THAT INCIDENT, TRY TO RECONNECT WITH THE PAIN YOU EXPERIENCED AT THAT MOMENT. TO HELP WITH THIS, MAKE YOUR DESCRIPTION AS DETAILED AS POSSIBLE.

4. THINK OF AN INCIDENT WHEN YOU WERE DEEPLY EMBARRASSED. TRY TO SEE THE PAIN YOU FELT FROM A POSITIVE POINT OF VIEW—AS A TOOL FOR *"FREEING YOURSELF FROM THE NEED TO INDULGE SELFISH DESIRES"*? TRY TO UNDERSTAND YOUR HURT AS A CHANCE TO MOVE CLOSER TO GOD'S ESSENCE. WRITE YOUR THOUGHTS BELOW.

5. HAVE YOU RECENTLY FELT DRIVEN OR OVERWHELMED BY THE NEED FOR SUCCESS, GRATIFICATION, OR CONTROL OVER OTHERS? WHAT DOES THAT NEED FEEL LIKE? HOW DID YOU FEEL ONCE THE INCIDENT THAT CAUSED THE NEED HAD PASSED? WHAT LESSONS DOES THIS TEACH YOU?

"TRANSFORMING INTO A BEING OF SHARING DOES NOT MEAN PERFORMING AN OCCASIONAL ACT OF GENEROSITY. IT MANDATES CONTINUAL CHANGE OF FORM: TO BECOME A BEING IN WHICH EVERY THOUGHT, EVERY ACTION, AND EVERY UTTERANCE COMES FROM THE DESIRE TO SHARE."

1. TRANSFORMATIVE SHARING MEANS GIVING OF YOUR-
SELF WHEN IT'S DIFFICULT OR EVEN PAINFUL TO DO SO.
IT REFERS TO ACTIONS OF SHARING THAT DON'T REIN-
FORCE THE EGO, BUT THAT <u>ATTACK</u> THE EGO AT ITS
DEEPEST FOUNDATIONS. WITH THIS IN MIND, DESCRIBE
SOME OPPORTUNITIES FOR TRANSFORMATIVE SHARING
IN THE RECENT PAST. HOW DID YOU RESPOND TO THOSE
OPPORTUNITIES? WHAT ARE YOUR FEELINGS ABOUT
THEM NOW?

2. *"BECOMING LIKE GOD IS A TWO-TIERED ASSAULT ON THE EGO: THE PROCESS OF DESTROYING THE INSIDE, AND PERFORMING ACTS OF SHARING ON THE OUTSIDE."*

WHAT ARE SOME POTENTIAL ACTS OF TRANSFORMATIVE SHARING THAT EXIST IN YOUR LIFE <u>RIGHT NOW</u>? IN THINKING ABOUT THESE OPPORTUNITIES, WHAT ARE YOUR THOUGHTS ABOUT THE DISCOMFORT THAT THEY WILL INCLUDE? HOW CAN YOU REASSURE YOURSELF THAT THIS DISCOMFORT IS A POSITIVE ATTRIBUTE IN THE PROCESS OF BECOMING LIKE GOD?

3. "WE SHARE WITH OTHERS SO WE CAN CONTINUALLY GIVE TO OURSELVES."

WHAT DOES THIS STATEMENT MEAN TO YOU? IN THE SPACE BELOW, USE ONE OR MORE INCIDENTS OF SHARING FROM YOUR RECENT LIFE TO ILLUSTRATE YOUR THOUGHTS.

4. THE JOURNEY TO GOD—AND TO TRANSFORMATIVE SHARING—IS AN EJECTION SEAT FROM THE COMFORT ZONE WE'RE USED TO."

WHAT COMFORT ZONES DO YOU INHABIT RIGHT NOW? WHAT CAN YOU DO TO MAKE YOURSELF UNDERCOMFORT-ABLE, NOT JUST FOR ITS OWN SAKE, BUT IN ORDER TO ENLARGE YOUR CAPACITY FOR SHARING AND BECOME MORE LIKE GOD?

5. *"EVERY IRRITATION IS A CHANCE TO EMBRACE DISCOMFORT AND CHIP AWAY ANOTHER ATOM OF EGO. EVERY ENCOUNTER IS ONE MORE CHANCE TO CONFRONT SELFISHNESS AND SHARE..."*

IN MANY AREAS OF OUR LIVES, THERE ARE THINGS THAT WE THINK WE OWN, BUT THEY REALLY OWN US. IN THE SPACE BELOW, LIST <u>FIVE</u> THINGS IN YOUR LIFE THAT YOU WOULD BE RELUCTANT TO GIVE OR SHARE WITH ANYONE ELSE.

IF YOU DID GIVE THEM AWAY, DESCRIBE THE FEELINGS YOU WOULD EXPERIENCE. CONSIDER THE POSSIBILITY THAT THE DISCOMFORT YOU MIGHT INITIALLY FEEL WOULD GIVE WAY TO A DEEPER SENSE OF LIBERATION. ALLOW YOURSELF TO EXPLORE THESE FEELINGS.

"CLARITY AND FOCUS ARE THE OPPONENT'S MORTAL ENEMIES. WE MUST FIGHT FOR CLARITY AT EVERY MOMENT: CLARITY ABOUT THE IMPORTANCE OF CLARITY, CLARITY THAT WE'RE IN A PRISON, CLARITY THAT WE'RE DESTINED TO BECOME LIKE GOD."

1. CLARITY MEANS RECOGNIZING THE STRUGGLE WE FACE AT EVERY MOMENT TO MOVE TOWARD THE ESSENCE OF GOD.

CHOOSE A SEEMINGLY UNIMPORTANT INCIDENT. DESCRIBE IT IN THE SPACE BELOW—AND AS YOU LOOK AT IT MORE CLOSELY, DESCRIBE WHAT SPECIFIC CHOICES YOU CAN MAKE EVEN IN THIS SEEMINGLY INSIGNIFICANT PART OF YOUR LIFE TO MOVE IN THE DIRECTION OF BECOMING LIKE GOD.

2. *"IF WE COULD SEE THAT EVERY ACTION ARISING FROM THE DESIRE TO RECEIVE FOR THE SELF ALONE HAS A NEGATIVE CONSEQUENCE, WE'D ARISE FROM OUR SLUMBER."*

IN LIGHT OF WHAT YOU KNOW ABOUT BECOMING LIKE GOD, WHAT ARE SOME NEGATIVE RESULTS OF YOUR EGO ACTIONS THAT WERE HIDDEN WHEN THEY TOOK PLACE, BUT ARE NOW CLEAR? WHAT INSIGHTS HAVE BROUGHT ABOUT THIS CHANGE?

80

3. WHAT ARE SOME SITUATIONS OF RELATIONSHIPS IN YOUR LIFE THAT SEEM UNCLEAR OR UNFOCUSED TO YOU? HOW CAN YOU CLARIFY THEM THROUGH YOUR UNDERSTANDING OF EGO, TRANSFORMATIVE SHARING, AND BECOMING LIKE GOD? WRITE YOUR THOUGHTS BELOW.

4. "THE ESSENCE OF THE EGO IS THE POWER TO CAUSE DOUBT..."

WHAT DOUBTS ARE PRESENT IN YOUR LIFE AT THIS MOMENT? WHAT ARE YOU CONFUSED ABOUT? WHAT ARE YOUR FEARS? WRITE YOUR THOUGHTS BELOW—AND AS YOU DO SO, RECOGNIZE THAT WHAT YOU FEEL IS NOTHING MORE THAT THE EGO TRYING ITS BEST TO SUBVERT YOUR POTENTIAL.

5. WITH AS MUCH CLARITY AS POSSIBLE, DESCRIBE THE ESSENCE OF GOD IN YOUR OWN WORDS. THEN DESCRIBE YOUR OWN ESSENCE AS IT SEEMS TO YOU RIGHT NOW: WHAT ARE THE POSITIVE AND NEGATIVE VALUES, BEHAVIORS, AND FEELINGS THAT MAKE YOU WHO YOU ARE? FINALLY, LIST SOME FOCUSED ACTIONS YOU CAN TAKE IMMEDIATELY TO BRIDGE THE GAP BETWEEN YOUR ESSENCE NOW AND YOUR DESTINY OF BECOMING LIKE GOD.

"IN ORDER FOR THE LIGHT
OF THE CREATOR TO BE
REVEALED, THERE MUST BE
A VESSEL TO RECEIVE IT.
THE NAME OF THAT VESSEL
IS CERTAINTY, AND THE
LEVEL OF LIGHT THAT IS
REVEALED DEPENDS ON THE
STRENGTH OF THAT
CERTAINTY."

1. CERTAINTY MEANS THAT WE KNOW IN OUR GUT THAT WE CAN BECOME LIKE GOD BECAUSE OUR ESSENCE IS GOD'S ESSENCE. GOD HAS PROVIDED US WITH ALL THE TOOLS WE NEED TO ACTUALIZE OUR POTENTIAL FOR GREATNESS.

WHAT GIFTS FROM THE CREATOR DO YOU HAVE? WHAT ARE THE WEAPONS YOU HAVE IN THE ONGOING WAR AGAINST YOUR EGO OPPONENT? DESCRIBE THEM IN THE SPACE BELOW, ALONG WITH CLEAR STEPS YOU CAN TAKE FOR PUTTING YOUR TOOLS INTO ACTION.

2. IN ADDITION TO KNOWING THAT WE <u>CAN</u> BECOME LIKE GOD, CERTAINTY ALSO INCLUDES THE KNOWLEDGE THAT WE <u>WILL</u> BECOME LIKE GOD. BUT IF YOU'RE LIKE MANY PEOPLE, THIS MAY SEEM LIKE A DIFFICULT IDEA TO GRASP. TO HELP WITH THIS, THINK OF SOME OTHER TIMES IN YOUR LIFE WHEN YOU HAD TROUBLE CONNECTING WITH THE REALITY OF AN EVENT THAT AT FIRST SEEMED FAR-FETCHED. WHEN YOU WERE IN NINTH GRADE, FOR INSTANCE, GRADUATING FROM HIGH SCHOOL MAY HAVE SEEMED ALMOST INCONCEIVABLE. LIST SOME OTHER EXAMPLES OF THIS KIND IN THE SPACE BELOW.

3. BELOW, LIST TEN THINGS THAT YOU <u>BELIEVE</u>. THEN LIST TEN OTHER THINGS OF WHICH YOU ARE TRULY <u>CERTAIN</u>. (EXAMPLE: "I BELIEVE IT WILL RAIN TODAY. I AM CERTAIN THAT I LIVE IN THE UNITED STATES.") BASED ON THE LISTS THAT YOU'VE CREATED, HOW WOULD YOU EXPLAIN THE DIFFERENCE BETWEEN BELIEF AND CERTAINTY IN THE SPIRITUAL REALM? WITH RESPECT TO BECOMING LIKE GOD, WHAT DO YOU BELIEVE, AND WHAT DO YOU <u>KNOW</u> WITH TOTAL CERTAINTY?

4. *"THE OPPONENT IS THE SOWER OF DOUBT. IN THE OPPONENT'S PARADIGM OF INSIGNIFICANCE, WE DON'T BECOME LIKE GOD BECAUSE WE BELIEVE WE <u>CAN'T</u> BECOME LIKE GOD."*

WHAT CAN YOU DO TO REPLACE THE BELIEF SYSTEM THE EGO IMPOSES ON YOU WITH CERTAINTY THAT BECOMING LIKE GOD IS ASSURED TO YOU? WHAT ACTIONS CAN YOU TAKE? WHAT SPIRITUAL TOOLS CAN YOU USE, SUCH AS PRAYER AND MEDITATION?

5. *"WHEN WE DON'T BELIEVE DEATH CAN BE OVER-COME, IT WILL NOT HAPPEN."*

KNOWLEDGE OF THE END OF DEATH IS THE ULTIMATE EXPRESSION OF CERTAINTY. WHAT ARE YOUR THOUGHTS ABOUT DEATH RIGHT NOW? DO YOU BELIEVE DEATH IS INEVITABLE, OR DO YOU BELIEVE THAT YOU HAVE THE POTENTIAL TO BRING ABOUT "THE DEATH OF DEATH"? HOW WILL YOUR LIFE CHANGE WHEN YOU BECOME CERTAIN THAT DEATH IS NOT YOUR ULTIMATE DESTINY?

"OUR TRANSFORMATION TO GOD IS THE ONLY WORTHWHILE GOAL IN LIFE. NOTHING LESS THAN COMPLETION OF THE JOURNEY WILL DO."

1. BASED ON WHAT YOU'VE LEARNED FROM READING BECOMING LIKE GOD, WRITE YOUR THOUGHTS ON THE DIFFERENCE BETWEEN "BEING A GOOD PERSON" AND BEING LIKE GOD. USE EXAMPLES FROM YOUR OWN LIFE TO CLARIFY YOUR THOUGHTS.

2. "THERE'S A TREASURE IN YOUR ATTIC, AND A LADDER WITH TEN RUNGS LEADING UP TO IT. IF YOU STOP AT THE NINTH RUNG, YOU MAY THINK YOU'VE COME VERY FAR. BUT YOU'VE GAINED NOTHING."

IN WHAT AREAS OF YOUR LIFE ARE YOU NOW ON "THE NINTH RUNG"? IN THOSE AREAS, WHAT SPECIFICALLY ARE YOU GOING TO DO TO TAKE THAT LAST ALL-IMPORTANT STEP?

3. *"THIS IS AN EXTRAORDINARY LESSON: FOR MOST OF US, BEING GOOD IS A BARRIER TO BECOMING LIKE GOD."*

IN THE SPACE BELOW, LIST SOME THINGS "GOOD" THINGS YOU'RE DOING RIGHT NOW THAT GIVE YOU COMFORT AND SATISFACTION. THEN LIST OTHER ACTIVITIES YOU COULD TAKE UP THAT WILL REALLY EXTEND YOURSELF IN THE DIRECTION OF BECOMING LIKE GOD. THINGS THAT WILL MAKE YOU UNCOMFORTABLE IN A POSITIVE WAY. THINGS THAT WILL NOT JUST MAKE YOU "GOOD," BUT WILL TRULY MAKE YOU <u>BETTER</u>.

4. THE GREAT KABBALIST RAV YEHUDA ASHLAG SAID THAT HIS GREATEST DISAPPOINTMENT WAS IN SEEING SOMEONE BEGIN ON THE PATH TOWARD BECOMING LIKE GOD, ONLY TO GIVE IT UP BEFORE COMPLETING THE TASK. WHAT KIND OF THINGS WOULD POTENTIALLY BLOCK YOU FROM COMPLETING THE JOURNEY? WRITE YOUR THOUGHTS BELOW.

5. WHAT THOUGHTS, PHRASES, OR INCIDENTS CAN YOU CALL UPON TO INSPIRE AND ENERGIZE YOURSELF ON THE PATH OF BECOMING LIKE GOD? LIST AS MANY OF THESE TOOLS AS YOU CAN IN THE SPACE BELOW. FEEL FREE TO USE MATERIAL FROM BOOKS, FILMS, OR THE LIVES OF OTHER PEOPLE, AS WELL AS FROM YOUR OWN EXPERIENCE.

"THE JOURNEY TO GOD IS A LIBERATION OF THE UNIFI-CATION WITH A MINUSCULE CORNER OF THE UNIVERSE CALLED [YOUR NAME HERE] TO UNIFICATION WITH LIVES EVERYWHERE."

1. *"COMPASSION IS NOT JUST A MATTER OF BEING NICE, SYMPATHETIC, AND GENEROUS. COMPASSION IS WHAT EMERGES FROM THE ASHES OF THE DESIRE TO RECEIVE FOR THE SELF ALONE WHEN, JUST AS EVERY BEING IS GOD'S BUSINESS, EVERY BEING BECOMES OUR BUSINESS AS WELL."*

DESCRIBE THREE SPECIFIC AREAS OF YOUR LIFE IN WHICH YOU CAN PUT THIS PRINCIPLE INTO ACTION.

2. THINK OF PEOPLE IN YOUR LIFE WHO TRULY EXTENDED THEMSELVES IN ORDER TO HELP YOU IN SOME WAY. DESCRIBE ONE OR MORE OF THESE PEOPLE BELOW— AND BE SURE TO EMPHASIZE THE DIFFICULTIES THEY MUST HAVE FACED IN BEING OF HELP TO YOU.

3. WHO ARE SOME PEOPLE FOR WHOM YOU CAN NOW EXPRESS COMPASSION? CAN YOU TRANSFORM THAT EXPRESSION INTO ACTION? DESCRIBE THEIR CIRCUMSTANCES IN AS MUCH DETAIL AS POSSIBLE, ALONG WITH THE POSITIVE SOLUTIONS YOU CAN HELP TO BRING ABOUT.

4. *"BECOMING LIKE GOD DEMANDS THAT WE END FOR-EVER EVERY DISTINCTION, BORDER, AND BOUNDARY BETWEEN WHAT IS US AND WHAT IS NOT US."*

IN YOUR OWN LIFE, WHAT ARE SOME BORDERS THAT WOULD BE TORN DOWN BY TRUE COMPASSION? HOW WOULD THE END OF THESE BORDERS CHANGE YOUR LIFE, AS WELL AS THE LIVES OF THOSE AROUND YOU?